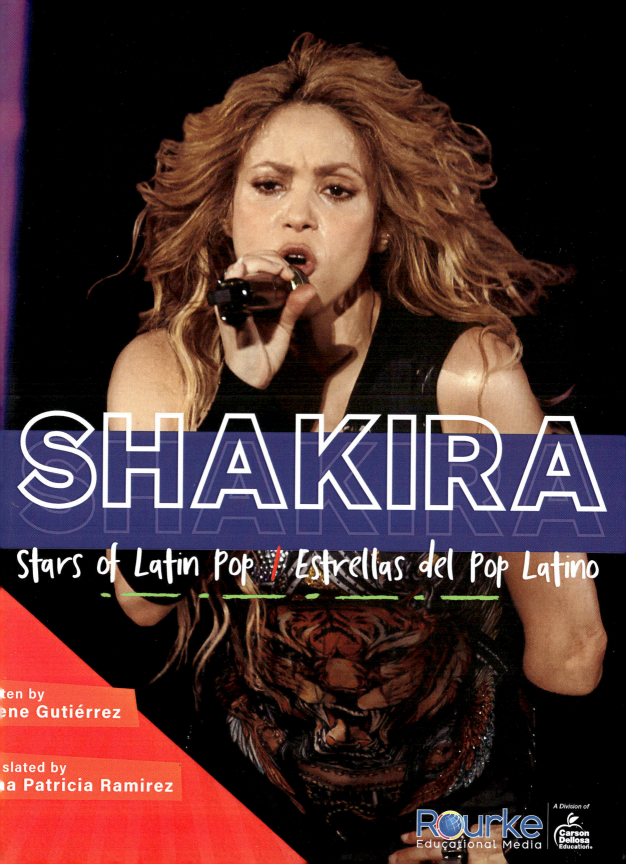

SHAKIRA

Stars of Latin Pop / Estrellas del Pop Latino

Written by
Irene Gutiérrez

Translated by
Ana Patricia Ramirez

Rourke
Educational Media

A Division of
Carson Dellosa Education

BEFORE AND DURING READING ACTIVITIES

Before Reading: *Building Background Knowledge and Vocabulary*

Building background knowledge can help children process new information and build upon what they already know. Before reading a book, it is important to tap into what children already know about the topic. This will help them develop their vocabulary and increase their reading comprehension.

Questions and Activities to Build Background Knowledge:

1. Look at the front cover of the book and read the title. What do you think this book will be about?
2. What do you already know about this topic?
3. Take a book walk and skim the pages. Look at the table of contents, photographs, captions, and bold words. Did these text features give you any information or predictions about what you will read in this book?

Vocabulary: *Vocabulary Is Key to Reading Comprehension*

Use the following directions to prompt a conversation about each word.
- Read the vocabulary words.
- What comes to mind when you see each word?
- What do you think each word means?

Vocabulary Words:
- charity
- contract
- crossover
- debut
- petition
- vibrato

Palabras del vocabulario
- caridad
- contrato
- debut
- fusión
- petición
- vibrato

During Reading: *Reading for Meaning and Understanding*

To achieve deep comprehension of a book, children are encouraged to use close reading strategies. During reading, it is important to have children stop and make connections. These connections result in deeper analysis and understanding of a book.

Close Reading a Text

During reading, have children stop and talk about the following:
- Any confusing parts
- Any unknown words
- Text to text, text to self, text to world connections
- The main idea in each chapter or heading

Encourage children to use context clues to determine the meaning of any unknown words. These strategies will help children learn to analyze the text more thoroughly as they read.

When you are finished reading this book, turn to the next-to-last page for After Reading Questions and an Activity.

Table of Contents

Tabla de contenido

Rising Star
Una estrella emergente

Shakira Isabel Mebarak Ripoll grew up in Barranquilla, Colombia. She began performing when she was four years old. She sang with a strong, loud voice. She taught herself to dance like the belly dancers from her father's home country of Lebanon.

• • •

Shakira Isabel Mebarak Ripoll creció en Barranquilla, Colombia. Comenzó a cantar cuando tenía cuatro años. Cantaba con una voz fuerte y alta. Aprendió sola a bailar como las bailarinas de vientre del país de su padre, Líbano.

Barranquilla

Venezuela

COLOMBIA

Ecuador

Peru

Shakira dreamed of being a writer. She got a typewriter on her eighth birthday and used it to write poems and songs. Then, she tried out for the school choir. The choir teacher told her he didn't want her in his choir. He said her **vibrato** sounded like the bleat of a goat.

• • •

Shakira soñaba con ser escritora. Le regalaron una máquina de escribir en su octavo cumpleaños y la usó para escribir poemas y canciones. Luego, se presentó a una audición para el coro de la escuela. El maestro del coro le dijo que no la quería en su coro. Le dijo que su **vibrato** sonaba como el balido de una cabra.

vibrato (vi-BRAH-toh): vibrating change of pitch in a voice or instrument

vibrato (vi-bra-to): cambio de tono por vibración en una voz o instrumento

Shakira's parents believed in her, though. Her mother took her to contests and auditions. When Shakira was 13, she signed her first **contract** with Sony Music Colombia. Shakira said, "I knew that I wanted to pursue a musical career, to sing for the rest of my life."

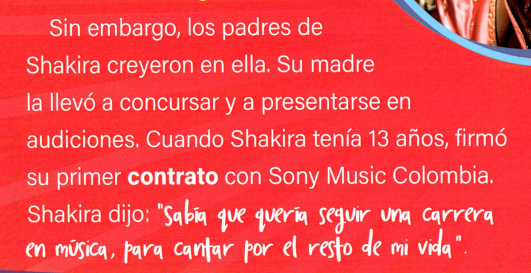

• • •

Sin embargo, los padres de Shakira creyeron en ella. Su madre la llevó a concursar y a presentarse en audiciones. Cuando Shakira tenía 13 años, firmó su primer **contrato** con Sony Music Colombia. Shakira dijo: "Sabía que quería seguir una carrera en música, para cantar por el resto de mi vida".

contract (kahn-trakt): a legal agreement between people, groups, or companies

contrato (con-tra-to): un acuerdo legal entre personas, grupos o compañías

Shakira with her parents, Mebarak Chadis and Nidia Ripoll Torrado.

Shakira con sus padres, Mebarak Chadis y Nidia Ripoll Torrado.

Family First

Shakira is the youngest child in her family. While growing up, her nine older half-siblings loved to see her sing and dance. Shakira's parents were proud of her powerful voice. Her family was involved in every step of her journey to fame.

● ● ●

La familia primero

Shakira es la más joven en su familia. Mientras crecía, a sus nueve medios hermanos mayores les gustaba verla cantar y bailar. Y los padres de Shakira estaban orgullosos de su potente voz. Su familia estuvo involucrada en cada paso de su camino hacia la fama.

9

Worldwide Superstar
Superestrella mundial

Shakira's **debut** album was called *Magia*. The album included the first song Shakira ever wrote, *Tus Gafas Oscuras*. She wrote the song when she was eight years old to honor her brother who died.

• • •

El álbum del **debut** de Shakira se llamó *Magia*. El álbum incluyó la primera canción que escribió Shakira, *Tus Gafas Oscuras*. Escribió la canción cuando tenía ocho años para honrar a su hermano que murió.

debut (DEY-byoo): the first time something happens or appears

debut (de-but): la primera vez que sucede o aparece algo

Shakira's first two albums did not sell many copies. Shakira didn't give up, though. She kept practicing and learned more about the music industry. It paid off! Her third album, *Pies Descalzos*, sold millions of copies.

• • •

Los dos primeros álbumes de Shakira no vendieron muchas copias. Sin embargo, Shakira no se dio por vencida. Siguió practicando y aprendiendo más acerca de la industria de la música. ¡Dio resultado! El tercer álbum *Pies Descalzos*, vendió millones de copias.

Got Goals?

Shakira worked hard to become famous. She said, "In this life, to earn your place you have to fight for it." What are your goals? How will you achieve them?

● ● ●

¿Estableció metas?

Shakira trabajó duro para volverse famosa. Ella dijo: "En esta vida, para ganarte un lugar tienes que pelear por él". ¿Cuáles son tus metas? ¿Cómo las lograrás?

Shakira was famous in Colombia. Then, she set a goal of singing around the world. She moved to the United States to learn English.

• • •

Shakira era famosa en Colombia. Luego, se puso la meta de cantar alrededor del mundo. Se mudó a Estados Unidos para aprender inglés.

Emilio and Gloria Estefan helped Shakira start her career in the U.S. Emilio was also Shakira's manage

Emilio y Gloria Estefan ayudaron a Shakira a comenzar su carrera en Estados Unidos. Emilio también el fue el represantante de Shakira.

English with the Estefans

Producer Emilio Estefan and musician Gloria Estefan saw Shakira's talent. They helped her learn to speak English. Shakira and Gloria wrote songs in English to tap into a new market.

● ● ●

Inglés con la familia Estefan

El productor Emilio Estefan y la cantante Gloria Estefan vieron el talento de Shakira. La ayudaron a aprender a hablar inglés. Shakira y Gloria escribieron canciones en inglés para entrar a un nuevo mercado.

This **crossover** artist has many talents. Shakira is fluent in six languages: Spanish, Portuguese, English, French, Italian, and Catalan. Her music has rock and roll, Middle Eastern, and Latin influences. She sings, dances, and even plays multiple instruments, such as the guitar, drums, and harmonica!

· · ·

Esta artista de **fusión** tiene muchos talentos. Shakira habla seis idiomas: español, portugués, inglés, francés, italiano y catalán. Su música tiene influencia del Rock and Roll, del medio oriente y latina. ¡Ella canta, baila e incluso toca varios instrumentos, como la guitarra, los tambores y la harmónica!

crossover (KROS-oh-ver): music or musicians liked by different audiences; often winning awards or being listed on different record charts

fusión (fu-sión): música o músicos que les gustan a diferentes audiencias, a menudo ganan premios o aparecen en diferentes listas de discos

Shakira has won hundreds of awards, including three Grammys and 12 Latin Grammys. She's even set Guinness World Records. One of the records she achieved was being the first person in the world with 100 million Facebook likes!

• • •

Shakira ha ganado cientos de premios, incluyendo tres Grammy y 12 Grammy latinos. Ella incluso estableció marcas mundiales de Guinness. ¡Una de sus marcas es ser la primera persona en el mundo con 100 millones de "me gusta" en Facebook!

In 2011, Shakira also won the Latin Recording Academy Person of the Year Award.

En 2011, Shakira también fue reconocida como la Persona del Año 2011 de La Academia Latina de Grabación.

Shakira is a well-celebrated superstar. In 2011, Shakira was given a star on the Hollywood Walk of Fame. She was a 2020 Super Bowl halftime show entertainer. Shakira is the only person to perform at three FIFA (Fédération Internationale de Football Association) World Cup Championships.

• • •

Shakira es una superestrella ampliamente reconocida. En 2011, a Shakira le dieron una estrella en el Paseo de la fama de Hollywood. Fue una de las artistas del medio tiempo del Supertazón en 2020. Shakira es la única persona que ha cantado en tres campeonatos mundiales de la FIFA (Federación Internacional de Fútbol Asociación).

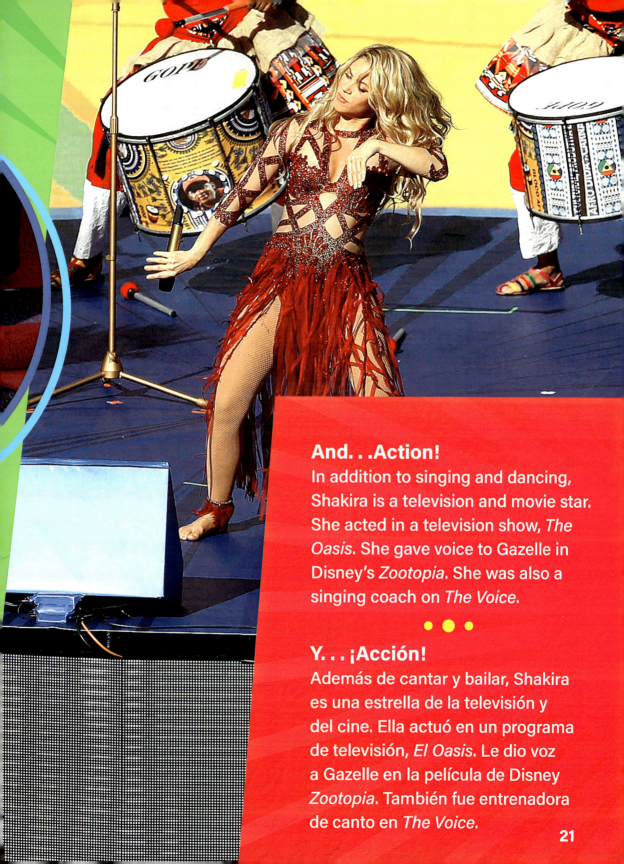

And. . .Action!

In addition to singing and dancing, Shakira is a television and movie star. She acted in a television show, *The Oasis*. She gave voice to Gazelle in Disney's *Zootopia*. She was also a singing coach on *The Voice*.

• • •

Y. . . ¡Acción!

Además de cantar y bailar, Shakira es una estrella de la televisión y del cine. Ella actuó en un programa de televisión, *El Oasis*. Le dio voz a Gazelle en la película de Disney *Zootopia*. También fue entrenadora de canto en *The Voice*.

21

Actions Offstage
Acciones fuera del escenario

When Shakira was young, she saw children without homes. Many of those children were trying to earn money for food. Most of them didn't go to school. Shakira knew she wanted to change things, but she wasn't sure how.

● ● ●

Cuando Shakira era joven vio a niños que no tenían hogar. Muchos de esos niños estaban tratando de ganar dinero para comer. La mayoría de ellos no iban a la escuela. Shakira sabía que quería cambiar las cosas, pero no estaba segura de cómo lo haría.

In 1995, Shakira formed The Barefoot Foundation to help all children go to school. Her **charity** has built seven schools. She has changed the lives of thousands of children in Colombia, South Africa, and Haiti. Shakira said, "A school opens, and the world changes."

• • •

En 1995, Shakira creó la fundación Pies Descalzos para ayudar a que todos los niños fueran a la escuela. Su fundación de **caridad** ha construido siete escuelas. Cambió las vidas de miles de niños en lugares como Colombia, Sudáfrica y Haití. Shakira dijo: "Una escuela abre y el mundo cambia".

charity (CHAIR-i-tee): an organization that helps others; or the act of giving

caridad (ca-ri-dad): una organización que ayuda a otros o el acto de dar

In 2003, Shakira became a UNICEF (United Nations Children's Fund) Goodwill Ambassador. In 2015, she delivered the #UpForSchool **petition** to the United Nations. More than 10 million people signed this form supporting schooling for all children.

● ● ●

En 2003, Shakira se convirtió en una embajadora de buena voluntad de UNICEF (Fondo de las Naciones Unidas para la Infancia). En 2015, entregó la **petición** de #UpForSchool a las Naciones Unidas. Más de 10 millones de personas firmaron este formulario apoyando que hubiera escuelas para todos los niños.

petition (puh-TI-shun): a document signed by people asking the government or groups to act on an issue

petición (pe-ti-ción): un documento firmado por las personas pidiendo al gobierno o a grupos que actúen en un asunto

Shakira has been honored around the world for her charity work. She has been given a United Nations Social Justice for Peace medal and the World Literacy Foundation's 2020 Global Literacy Award. Shakira said that helping educate children is "one of the most rewarding things I've done in my lifetime."

• • •

Shakira ha sido honrada alrededor del mundo por su trabajo caritativo. Ganó la medalla de Justicia Social para la Paz de las Naciones Unidas en 2010; y en 2020, el Premio de Alfabetización de la Fundación Mundial para la Alfabetización. Shakira dijo que ayudar a educar a los niños es "una de las cosas más gratificantes que he hecho en mi vida".

Helping Others

Shakira said, "I trust that as time goes by, there will be more and more people who want to help those in need. When that happens, the world will definitely come to know peace." What are you doing to help others?

● ● ●

Ayudando a otras personas

Shakira dijo: "Confío que conforme pase el tiempo, habrá más y más personas que quieran ayudar a aquellos que lo necesiten. Cuando esto suceda, el mundo definitivamente conocerá la paz". ¿Qué estás haciendo para ayudar a otras personas?

Index

After - Reading Questions

1. How do you think Shakira's childhood impacted her rise to fame?

2. How did learning English change Shakira's life?

3. What are some of Shakira's talents?

4. What challenges or setbacks did Shakira face in her life?

5. Why do you think helping children is important to Shakira?

Activity

Shakira has been performing and helping others for most of her life. What do you love to do? How might you help others? Write a letter and/or draw pictures to your future adult self. Tell yourself about your future plans and what you hope to do to make the world a better place

Índice

Preguntas para después de la lectura

1. ¿Cómo crees que la infancia de Shakira impactó su ascenso hacia la fama?

2. ¿Cómo cambió la vida de Shakira cuando aprendió inglés?

3. ¿Cuáles son algunos de los talentos de Shakira?

4. ¿Qué retos o reveses enfrentó Shakira en su vida?

5. ¿Por qué crees que ayudar a los niños es importante para Shakira?

Actividad

Shakira ha estado cantando y ayudando a otras personas la mayor parte de su vida. ¿Qué te gusta hacer? ¿Cómo podrías ayudar a otras personas? Escribe una carta o haz dibujos para cuando seas adulto en el futuro. Habla de tus planes futuros y lo que esperas hacer para que el mundo sea un mejor lugar.

About the Author
Sobre la autora

Like Shakira, Jolene Gutiérrez loves to sing! She also believes strongly in education for all and works as a teacher-librarian in Denver, Colorado. Connecting students with books and sharing information are some of her favorite things. Learn more about Jolene, her writing, and her dreams at **www. jolenegutierrez.com.**

• • •

Jolene trabaja como maestra y bibliotecaria en una escuela en Denver, Colorado. Conectar a los estudiantes con libros y compartir información son algunas de las cosas favoritas de Jolene. Obtén más información sobre Jolene, sus escritos y sus sueños en www.jolenegutierrez.com.

QUOTE SOURCE: @katiecouric: Shakira. (2009, December 1). YouTube. https://www.youtube.com/watch?v=jM7-MiWYKt0&feature=emb_rel_end. Diego, Ximena. Shakira: Woman Full of Grace. New York: Fireside, 2001. "Shakira." Shakira. Accessed May 13, 2020. https://www.shakira.com/. Shakira. (2019, November 23). Shakira's speech at #WISE19 (Qatar). YouTube. https://www.youtube.com/watch?list=RDCMUCYLNGLIzMhRTi6ZOLjAPSmw&v=8AdpYxq4QrY&feature=emb_rel_end. The Editors of Encyclopaedia Britannica. (2020, March 12). Shakira. Retrieved from https://www.britannica.com/biography/Shakira.

PHOTO CREDITS: page 5: ©Petr Toman / Shutterstock, ©Olga Turkas; page 6: ©MIKE BLAKE / NEWSCOM; page 7: ©Katarzyna Bialasiewicz Photographee.eu /Getty Images/iStockphoto; page 9: ©Leonard Zhukovsky / Shutterstock; page 10-11: ©Richard Ulreich / ZUMAPRESS.com/Newscom; page 12: ©Anna Kim / Getty Images/iStockphoto, ©Karen I. Hirsch / ZUMAPRESS/Newscom; page 14-15: ©marchello74; page 15: ©Petr Toman / Shutterstock.com, ©Leonard Zhukovsky / Shutterstock.com; page 16: ©Petr Toman / Shutterstock.com; page 17: ©Leonard Zhukovsky / Shutterstock; page 18-19: © Represented by ZUMA Press, Inc.; page 20-21: ©Marijan Murat / dpa / Newscom; page 21: © Represented by ZUMA Press, Inc.; page 22-23: REUTERS /Newscom, ©Kyodo / Newscom; page 23: ©Melissa J. Perenson / ZUMAPRESS.com / Newscom; page 25: ©Featureflash Photo Agency / Shutterstock; page 26: © Represented by ZUMA Press, Inc.; page 27: ©Brendan McDermid / REUTERS / Newscom; page 28: © Represented by ZUMA Press, Inc.; page 29: ©Yohei Osada / AFLO / Newscom

Library of Congress PCN Data

Shakira / Jolene Gutiérrez
(Stars of Latin Pop)
ISBN 978-1-73164-335-3 (hard cover)
ISBN 978-1-73164-299-8 (soft cover)
ISBN 978-1-73164-367-4 (e-Book)
ISBN 978-1-73164-399-5 (ePub)
Library of Congress Control Number: 2020945043

Rourke Educational Media
Printed in the United States of America
05-1002311948

Edited by: Madison Capitano
Cover design by: Michelle Rutschilling
Interior design by: Book Buddy Media